Merry Christmas Darling

Poetry Collection

*Filled with
Faith, Hope and Love*

annette journet jaco

Have A Merry Christmas Darling Poetry Collection: Filled with Faith, Hope and Love-by Annette Journet Jaco.

Copyright-2017 by Annette Journet Jaco.
No part of this book may be copied or reproduced in any form or manner except with the written permission of the author of this work.

Printed in the United States of America.

Spread the joy of this holiday season with poetry!

CONTENTS:

The Carols

Some Silver, Some Gold

Fireplace Fire

Jesus Season

True Love

Love This Christmas

First Dance

My Love Is Here

First Christmas

Peeking

Picnic Basket

Lessons

Noise

Apple Pie

Mama's Tree

Young Mother

Young Love Goes Shopping

All About Love

Stockings Hang

Brother Loves

Daddy I Miss You

Drum

Red Is Seasonal

Merry Christmas Darling

Believing Season

It Was A Cold Night

Sister, Sister Bond

Mistletoe Kiss

Joy Is Better

Tears Flow

Seasonal Love

Christmas And Pecans

Adoption

Frail Child

Smile

Missed Love

So Fragile

My Off Sweaters

Engagement

Big City Dreams

Lonely Elders

Rainy Day

Christmas Hat

Born

Happy Tears

Midnight

Tickles

The singing is glorious and the praises are great. Giving glory unto the Lord, singing carols like we used to.

The Carols

The singing is glorious, praising our Father.
Celebrating the season, giving honor to Him.
Singing, birth of the Son of God is wonderful.
Jesus is born, the carols are sung wonderfully.
Sing oh ye merry gentlemen and women; sing.
For the Lord is wonderful and mighty so sing.
Around the corner some see a group singing.
Going to go caroling, yet mostly in the movies.
The things that were once so normal are not.
Caroling comes around the Christmas holiday.
So they never grow old. Give honor today.
It is the season to give glory, it's Christmas.
The Savior was born on Christmas day.

We have some in silver and some dressed in gold. The beautiful decorations remind us of home, during this wonderful season of grandeur.

Some Silver, Some Gold

Everything is green all over the land.
The decorations, the trees, the wreath.
All is so flourishing, lavished in green.
The pine needles on the living room floor.
On thing for sure, there is silver and gold.
The garlands in the kitchen and on the tree.
Over doors inside and out, filled with green.
Let's dress with a little silver and some gold.

The wood is burning in the fireplace and the room is warm and it is glowing. We are warm and happy around the fire during this wonderful season.

Fireplace Fire

Flames glowing, crisp wood burns.
Eyes sparkle, this day, its warmth.
It's a day to open gifts, and to pray.
It is a season to give and to say.
God is love, love is in the universe.
There was a day long ago; a birth.
The birth of a Savior, joy and mirth.
We have to gladly celebrate Jesus.
It's a very merry Christmas! Jesus.

Jesus is always the reason and will always be. He is the way and the truth for all seasons.

Jesus Season

Don't put the x. Not the way.
Jesus is the reason for this.
Jesus was born in a manger.
There was a reason for this.
Eloquence in speech, a child.
Grew in stature from a child.
Born of a virgin for a reason.
He did come for this season.
Born to be Jesus our Savior.
Came to die, to let us know.
We are here and there is hope.
No x; just Jesus. He is Christmas.
C.H.R.I.S.T. is Christmas, Preach!

Remember to always say, I love you!

True Love

True love is simply fresh, never old.
It is something that anger ignores.
Loving words says always, I love you.
True love wants the company of two.
Not holding grudges, not being raw.
Loving someone is being able to talk.
Never saying I hate you, never ever.
True love says I love you, always.

This is the meaning to give these gifts. Love when we give on this wonderful day. Adapt to change and give always!

Love This Christmas

Unwrap the great presents but don't forget
to send love this special day; this Christmas.
Tell your loved ones how much they mean to
you because this is the meaning of Christmas.
We live on borrowed time and we have to pray.
God gave us this holy season to say thank you.
So don't forget to love this Christmas season.
It's a wonderful time; love is fragrant in the air!

Yes, my Lord kept me in the strange ways of the day and night. He kept me! I can dance and sing praises to Him every day. Sending my praises up!

First Dance

Only three, in his arms.
Strong and bold, I sleep.
Strong moves of his feet.
Dancing for me, as I sleep.
In his arms, I'm comforted.
There are classical sounds.
Murmurs here, there, chirps.
Outside noise, the music stops.
Hearing as I was sound asleep.
In his arms, my Savior kept me.
I was safe and the music was soft.
Atmospheric quivers are normal.
Quiet again, singing, morning again.
My Father kept me. He kept me!

Lovers come to visit on the holidays. They take some special time off being considerate for their loved one. Celebrate; your love is here.

My Love Is Here

Come to visit this time of year.
My love comes, my love is here.
It's a time that I wait for him here.
My homeland he comes calling here.
Once a year, once a year, he's here.
A good friend, a distant love child.
Friends forever and ever, a love.
Two souls happy this time of year.
So happy my love is here, he's here.

Baby's first steps and first Christmas is a lovely time of the year. It is marvelous and unforgettable.

First Christmas

Tippy toe to the pretty Christmas tree.
It sits in the mere center of the room.
There is a gift for baby, tiny little bay.
First steps, understanding, giggles.
Tippy toe little one near the big tree.
Then turns to look at joyful mommy.
See daddy dressed in odd clothing.
Babies wondering, is this gift for me?
They didn't actually realize at the time.
The gift that truly mattered was love.
The huge hugs from family and smiles.
Feeling safe, prayers, tucked into bed.
Protective daddy; mega santa on sled.
Mommy's sweet kisses, protects us.
First Christmas and many small gifts.
So be thankful, don't forget to pray...

The children are excitingly waiting to receive their gifts on the night before Christmas. Adults remember when they themselves were tiny tots. It is such a special night.

Peeking

Children want to know about their gifts.
They ask and mama says don't worry.
It's just the night before Christmas.
So they sleep and wait and they peek.
Hoping to see a great big guy in a suit.
What is the meaning of the real truth?
Jesus is the meaning of why we give.
We give to celebrate His birth, so give.

Always give to the orphans, because they have no parents. Remember that their semblance of family is quite different so show them compassion. Fill their basket!

Picnic Basket

Children receive toys around the holidays.
The orphans, the poor, the less fortunate.
Can we make sure that we fill their basket?
A basket for someone in need, this Christmas.
Children and family are happy but the homeless
might be looking for a dream blessing or miracle.
So make a picnic basket with fruits and whistles.
The situations so unique; fatherless, motherless.
The children were missing out on something.
So let's fill a picnic basket for someone in need.
Say a prayer this wonderful holiday season.

Pray for the child who is alone this holiday season and every holiday. Pray for them every day and help them to make honorable friends.

Lessons

Standing under a big old tree.
She did not want to approach.
Other kids playing tag, pushing.
Running, rushing; laughing loud.
So she kept her stance, silent.
No, I don't want to go said mind.
I would rather stay here, please.
Right here with my tree, please.
For I know who is always with me.
Then another girl says to her.
Want to play? Try a cartwheel.
Didn't quite get right, she quits.
Near that old wood oak she stood.
In silent peace she prays, help me.
"Help me to make it this day Lord,
I want to go home please, Lord."
Tomorrow is Christmas. Finally!

We want the noises to stop and we seek peace this holiday season. I pray for peace.

Noise

Noises, cracking sounds then peace.
In her mind she heard the invader.
Just a sound; it was not an alien.
Why wouldn't it go away please?
In the classroom teacher speaks.
She could not hear her own voice.
The sound was loud, not her choice.
In anxiety, she puts her hands together.
In a silent prayer all through the day.
Praying to her Father, help it go away.
So God answers her prayers today.
Time for the holidays, can't wait.

The juicy apple pie that grandmother bakes is so hot and steamy from the oven and it will taste so good on this Christmas.

Apple Pie

Grandma stands in her fragrant kitchen.
In her green apron she constantly taps.
Her granddaughter's hand, favor, slaps.
Smiling down at her, teasing with her eyes.
Grandma making crispiest, tasty apple pies.
It was right around the Christmas season.
So hold on just one minute! Christmas pies?
This grandmother did not need a reason.
She enjoyed her grandchildren and baking.
Especially around the happy holiday season.
Carefully curling the top crust into a design.
She worked, putting in the sweet apple filling.
Nicely leaving some on a spoon for the kids.
It was her joy to see such glee on that face.
Baby's faces smiling; making good apple pie.

This year's tree does not have to be expensive. Cut a pine tree from the yard. Mama's tree was so unique.

Mama's Tree

One winter day daddy arrived home early.
Mama wants a Christmas tree from a field?
Daddy went to chop down a soft green pine.
A sprinkling sparkly evergreen was so fine.
A bit imperfect and lacking enchantment!
But it would do just fine for the children!
Daddy marched over the fields with a cane.
He chopped down one of the sprawling trees.
He came home marching and dragging a tree.
Tediously and gleefully they decorated a tree.
With paper made school decorations and lights.
Elated children stood near the Christmas tree;
Yes, the smallest child put the angel on top!

Bless a young mother this year. Give and it shall be given. The kids need to have a special holiday so it is all given to the children.

Young Mother

Twenty two with two kids is a young mother.
Christmas season is in the cold of winter.
The children's coats are ridiculously bulky.
Cold and crisp holidays bring a good cheer.
Mother still frets, children need new coats.
Will the children have most of their wishes?
This Christmas there's a long awaited list.
It could be a batman toy or a Barbie doll.
It's all so meaningless except to a kid.
So mother kneels; says a silent prayer.
She knows her part time job isn't enough.
She knows her husband brings in little.
She realizes her strength is in praying.
She knows her God and His faithfulness.
Every year God comes through her faith.
God is in control in her life so it's all good.

Walking in the mall shopping for the right gift is the young couple. It can be a cookie or something to wear. It is a great time for great love.

Young Love Goes Shopping

Malls are plentiful, lovely cookies for Christmas.
Smells so strong and the sugar is so different.
Sweet and so good like the season is so holly.
Can we feel Christmas everyday? We could!
Celebrating the joy of giving is grand and nice.
Just say a prayer throughout the day, twice.
The season for givers is filled with spice.
So continue to flourish and go out to shop.
It is that time of year, so pray don't stop.
Young love going shopping after a prayer.
Givers are praying to find a gift for someone.

The holiday season is all about love; so is every other day.
Spread the love!

All About Love

It's love in the air. It's a feeling.
It's surreal. Love is God. God is love.
Let's enjoy this love so powerful.
The love of our Father is full of love.
The love of our God is extra real.
Sing a sweet lullaby to the children.
Kiss them goodnight, hold them.
Wait for a sign of love in the air.
Tomorrow is Christmas. Yes!
Have a love filled Christmas.
It's all about love, all about love.

Christmas stockings are so symbolic. Don't forget to give out a Christmas stocking filled with goodies this year.

Stockings Hang

Over the fireplace stockings hang.
Sometimes they are over our bed.
One eye open throughout the night.
Can't even get a shut eye little child.
Over the mantel the stockings hang.
Waiting for moms to drop in the gifts.
Putting joy and long smiles for the kids.
Waking to a gleeful morning is the child.
Checking each stocking is the child.
It's a very exciting time for the child.

Never forget to take the opportunity to say you love someone and that you thank them. Love your family every day.

Brother Loves

He is in Heaven gone away.
Brother was here, gone away.
Prayers for times we had together.
It was today, tomorrow then now.
Now he is gone but he loves on.
He is with Jesus so he loves.
Surrounded by God, he loves.
He continues to love us, we him.
Love never dies. It never dies.
Love them now while they are here.
Love your brother who is not here.
He is in Heaven with Jesus.
This Christmas he is missed.
He is in Heaven with Jesus.

Cherish your dad this holiday. He is special because God gave him to you. Wish your dad a happy holiday.

Daddy I Miss You

The greatest pop he could have been.
He was the only dad that could be.
Flawed as we all are, largely was he.
So forgive what he was lacking, see.
He was just a man with his own plan.
He had things to do sometimes away.
Sometimes it didn't include the children.
Still daddy is missed around the season.
He walked on occasions carrying groceries.
No car, just two feet and a meal for the family.
Daddy is missed. Sometimes daddy tried to be fair.
He was not perfect but sometimes he was there.
Daddy was married thirty five years or more.
Mom was his love for thirty five years or more.

Our hearts are beating like a drum to the worship music.
Sing and enjoy the holiday and beat your drum.

Drum

Hit the sticks together, drum.
Drum for the holiday, drum.
This is a cause to celebrate.
Drum, drum; hit on the sticks.
Sing a mother's prayer today.
Songs will praise the Savior.
Listen to the sounds of angels.
Listen to the silent nights, days.
Time is approaching a New Year.
Daddy's prayers answered today.
Everyone is together and gleeful.
Enjoy the seasons, we have today.

Wrapping paper is very personal. Pink or blue, red or your favorite combinations of colors are your choice. Choose red for this season.

Red Is Seasonal

We see the suits and the wrapping paper.
All things red and green; colors are bright.
This is how it is done, every year is bright.
Songs so light and merry, the red is red.
Don't forget to pray for the crimson red.
Strength is vibrant love; a bold meaning.
It's seasonal, it's strong and it is merry.

It is time again for the Christmas ball. Don't forget your shiny attire and enjoy your celebration.

Merry Christmas Darling

Excitement and celebration is in the air.
Shiny gowns are unwrinkled, in the air.
Times for getting together to celebrate.
Rooms are booked, people are hurrying.
Iron your rags, traffic is hurried and huge.
Nerves are cracking, Merry Christmas.
Her date arrives and he rings the bell.
She opens the door and he looks great.
She has on a lavish gown, greetings darling.
It's a most beautiful time, and they drive off.
The night is slowly going by, toasts everywhere.
Merry Christmas don't forget why we are here.
Don't forget darling, have a Merry Christmas.

It is time to exercise our faith during the believing season. It is time to have faith every day throughout the year. Have faith!

Believing Season

Is there a time to start believing?
Should I wait for the season?
Must we not believe the time?
Times we spend together so fine.
Times are magical, they are real.
So believe in miracles, we are here.
Don't wait for the season to believe.
Faith starts at the beginning, believe.
As a child who is taught as a baby.
He trusts and believes his parents.
Just trust and believe in the Savior.

Jesus was born in this beautiful time. We celebrate His birth and the wise men did travel to bring Him gifts of gold, frankincense, and myrrh. We celebrate because of Jesus Christ.

It Was A Cold Night

Mom made quilts together of old cloth.
The house was cold, there was no heat.
Only a gas stove and a space heater.
It was a cold, dark and lengthy night.
A miracle baby born on a cold night.
Winter, the big North Star did shine.
Men led to see a beauty of wonder.
Beauty so real, magnificent in baby.
A real cold night so beautiful, a baby.
Enjoy what you have, absorb the moment.
It's a beautiful time to share our moments.

The holiday is a time of memories that we make and that we have made. Celebrate your sister bond this season.

Sister, Sister Bond

Ponytails combed neat by mom.
Two girls close in age and height.
They get their makeover each morning.
Sometimes up to six ponytails for school.
The sister, sister bond is somewhat great.
Its Christmas morning and the presents
are underneath the lovely Christmas tree.
Oh, no what am I getting this time, socks?
Sisters share a glance both eyes popping.
Disappointed by socks, maybe a weird toy!
Oh, no sister, sister bond was so strong.
Up until this Christmas morning it broke!
One is not happy and the other is stoked.

Don't ever give up on love especially during the holidays. Love your special person and celebrate the coming year!

Mistletoe Kiss

She's single and free, dressed for the season.
Silver and gold worn, three friends are meeting.
Girls looking great sharing happiness and cheer.
One girl single, other two girls have someone near.
Still a single woman and the New Year is rolling in.
Mistletoe kiss who will she find? How awkward it is.
She entertains slipping to another room, have a fizz.
Five, four, three, two, one! Here comes a new kiss.
He notices her glitter and how her eyes sparkle.
He stands near her, and right on one they kiss.
Never give up on love, during this season's bliss.

Pray for the white Christmas, snow is coming soon. In the south and the north, it is always a welcoming surprise. Enjoy a white Christmas.

Joy Is Better

We woke up to snow on the ground.
In the south town snow was all around.
Whew! What a wonder and a joy.
It was around the holidays, o boy!
A miracle, a quiet night, not a sound.
Christmas night with the kids; joy is abound.
Sound asleep they were at midnight until morning.
Opening gifts only to find a winter white glow.
On the ground on Christmas day, big snow.
What a grand miracle and a picturesque view.
Happy holidays this year to you!

Enjoy the time in happiness and good cheer. We may even shed a tear of joy. It is a glorious time.

Tears Flow

A love song is sung during the season.
A class act, a turn around for people.
The song was dedicated to those we love.
It was about our Savior above. He is love.
Whatever might be going wrong on tonight,
take a moment to praise Him for awhile.
It is for a reason that we gleefully sing.
The sacrifice so mighty with flowing tears.
Can you shed a tear for the season this year?
You would if only you understood the reason.
Sing and let it drip, don't be shy; cry for Him.
I will cry too, so let's let love hugely abide.
Let the tears flow, please let the tears flow.
It is time to celebrate the Savior Jesus.

Feel the sensations and good spirit. Love is in the air and we will always feel this godly love in this time.

Sensational Love

Love was plentiful and great this year.
There were times of grief but do not fear.
There were shootings and cars plowing.
There were private places awfully invaded.
So awful and calculated, but let love flow.
Let it flow and let love win, sensational love.
It is a season to celebrate; certainty and hope.
Pray for that sensational blessing and love.
God is waiting for the invitation, He is waiting.
Surrender to sensational love, hate will succumb.
Love will win, love always wins; sensational love.

I love to pick them up, these great big pecans. Underneath the trees and then bring them in and make a great and tasty pecan pie.

Christmas And Pecans

So many pecans underneath the pecan tree.
Having to bend to pick them up oh, gosh, gee.
Not much joy during this hard autumn but wait.
Joy is a coming after peeling and it's all baked.
The pies coming out of the oven, smells great.
There were times like those when Christmas,
and delicious pecans went together. The turkey,
the pies, the work and the washing of hands.
What a wonderful plan of the Almighty God.
Sometimes it's all in the cooking and grace.
Thanking God for all the blessings in our place.

Put joy and glee in someone's heart. Adopt if you can. It is a huge sacrifice. This is a time of giving.

Adoption

A child is patiently waiting since Thanksgiving.
She wants a phone call or a visit from family.
There is no one. She was given away at birth.
It's a difficult time. The season has come again.
This home where she resides is new. She prays.
Someday she will be able to break some rules.
Accustomed to times and schedules in places.
One day she will have a job and her own place.
Since the time her mama gave her away she waits..
Wanting to belong and she will because she prays.
She found Jesus and He invited her in, He stays.
He never leaves like others once did. Jesus stays.

Feed a hungry child during the holiday season and every day. It is a time to make sure others are enjoying Christmas and bringing in a happy New Year.

Frail Child

Frail child lost and weary in his mother's arms;
nothing to do but sit on her lap, no real floor.
He longs for a small meal a day, hopefully.
Why can't she just feed me or not give birth?
Born to suffer; succumbing to less worth.
Can we think about him during the season?
Can we be thankful that we are blessed?
Some children suffer and they are frail.
The lost weak mother waits and waits.
The hungry children need a meal today.
A better day they dream of, so just pray.
Be thankful that your needs are met today.
Give to the less fortunate, on this holiday.

It is good to wish everyone a season's greetings this holiday season. Remember to always smile.

Smile

Smile with one, season's greetings.
Wish someone well; extend greetings.
Don't pass up an acquaintance.
A patron you can be, so give.
Give a smile, a blessing, a gift.
Wish someone well; extend greetings.

We must remember those that we lost especially during the holidays and always smile and know that they are in a better and happier existence.

Missed Love

When I think about the overwhelming love
of a wonderful young brother who is missed.
At the next thought, I think of a God who gives.
It's sad to see one go; He promised us a place to go.
My heart knows there's a mansion in the sky so grand.
I know he walks there on green grass. I know he stands.
Or better he is daily walking perhaps on streets of gold.
Yes he is dearly missed; so missed this loved one oh, oh.
He walks on brass in a huge mansion; on streets of gold.

We must celebrate the one who makes us strong. Jesus was sent for mankind by a Father who cares. God is our strength.

So Fragile

Fragile is the man or the woman.
There is such fragility in this world.
So much is happening, so fragile.
What matters is not about the fragile.
It is about the strong who overcome;
the God who lives in us who says come.
Lord you are strong when we are weak.
So fragile we have been but now we see.
We see a world so broken, so full of faith.

It is time to wear the pretty and the ugly Christmas sweaters. Celebrate and be in good cheer and dress for the occasion.

My Off Sweaters

Off and on are the sweaters I wear.
Winter has come again, oh I swear.
This snow comes down after much sun.
I will be so gleeful and times that shun
us becomes times to celebrate, have fun.
Knit a sweater this Christmas, sit, have fun.
Kindred spirits sing a little jingle, joke.
Have some eggnog and remain stoked.
It's the Christmas sweater so warm indeed.
Have a happy sweater and enjoy them please.
Happy Holidays!

This is the best time of the year for engagement. A lovely man gives a lovely woman a diamond.

Engagement

I saw it in the glass case.
I was visiting the jeweler.
I was in a lovely dress shop.
Then I stopped on the way out.
It's a new season and I dream.
My desire for this Christmas I see.
It's glowing brightly in front of me.
Engaging with this sight unforeseen.
A shining star. A sprinkling diamond.
A true vision underneath a green tree.

Missing someone at Christmas is one of the things we fear, but saying a prayer and visiting when we can is always dear. Live your big city dreams!

Big City Dreams

Walking downtown like I dreamed.
I felt someone brush me on my way.
Bags filled with the big names, silk.
I'm walking on the avenue, a model.
Catching a show later, or the opera.
It's perfect, the dinner with a client.
Later I'm missing family from afar.
I book a train the next day to board.
Lonely in a big city dream is boring.
Going to see mother for Christmas.
Much better than a big city dream.

Never forget the elders; they always pray for their families. Always pop in and visit the elders.

Lonely Elders

The truth has to be recognized.
Their lives must be recognized.
They are lonely people, elders.
They have done so much for us.
We must not forget the sacrifice.
Cooking by the stove, laughing.
Hugs and a kiss on the cheek.
We must never forget to speak.
Tell them hello, extend a hand.
They were here first, were next.
Be kind this Christmas, to elders.

Celebrate the rain; the ground is cleansed. The air is fresh and everything feels awakened. It is a rainy season but celebrate.

Rainy Day

Lonely day it is pouring down.
Is anyone coming over today?
Last year not a soul arrived,
late in the evening, surprise.
How can this be Christmas?
How can this be a joyous day?
Open your Bible and give thanks.
No one comes early but Jesus is.
He is already with you, Jesus is.
If a soul arrives or not don't cry.
You might be last on their agenda.
Put God first, sing carols; smile.

Put on your hat and drink some cocoa. It feels like Christmas!

Christmas Hat

Sipping on hot chocolate in a santa hat.
Singing contemporary Christian songs.
A little jingle bells and some silent night.
Who wears their hideous pajamas tonight?
Or perhaps while sipping on cocoa chanting,
praising those humungous holiday sweaters.
Who has the worst looking sweater? Who?
Can we walk in those Christmas socks?
Sitting and roasting by the fire place.
It truly is a nice white Christmas in a hat.
So wear it well and be warm. Good wishes.

We celebrate our one and only Savior. That is what Christmas is all about, but not only Christmas. Every day we must give praises unto God.

Born

He was born in a manger.
Sweet child for the world.
He was sent to save us, us.
How grand the gifts of mirth.
Jesus was born, it's jubilant.
Hurrah! Praises! Jubilance!
The big star was bright afar.
The wise gentlemen seeking.
The night so bright and meek.
Their worship was so great!
Glory to the Highest! Great!
He was born. Born!

Have tears of happiness and think about the good old days. There are so many ways to celebrate and to remember the good times.

Happy Tears

I remember him who was once here.
A relative who is gone now, was here.
His flesh, we touch; hugs and smiles.
Around this Happy New Year smiles.
We celebrate, we think of those lost.
I cry tears, tears painful and so sad.
Heaven is where we will go; ironclad.
Heaven is where we go. Happy tears.

The clock strikes at the midnight hour. The bells ring. It is a time to look forward to. The children are happy. Christmas has now come in the wee hours of the morning. It is a good time.

Midnight

Children love to wait.
They love to say midnight.
Midnight is when they wait.
For those who believe in chimneys.
They wait to see who eats the cookie.
Children love to wait impatiently.
A toy in a stocking over the fireplace.
A toy underneath a big tree stays.
Until morning when kids fall asleep.
The anticipation over midnight.
Yet they fall asleep before midnight.
In anticipation for a small toy.
They fall asleep before midnight.

Enjoy your time with relatives. Enjoy your time with your grandparents. It is a favorite time of the year.

Tickles

Tickles from grandma and grandpa.
Little grandchildren love to laugh.
Spending a night waiting for tickles.
What is it that they love so much?
They love grandma and grandpa.
Buckets of smiles, favor and love.
It's a holiday love from above.
Spending time with grandparents.

Annette Journet Jaco Poetry Books

Songs & Whispers
A Song From Eden
Sing Lover Of My Soul
Children Let's Sing Hallelujah
Beautiful Poetry For Women: Jewel In The Hand Of God: 20 Breathtaking Poems
Beautiful Woman: What A Diadem You Are: Quotes and Poems For Encouragement
Fresh Water: Life After Domestic Violence and the Anointed Life in You: 20 Refreshing Poems
Beautiful Mothers Day Poetry: Celebrating Moms
When The Rain Falls God Dries My Tears: Cancer Prayers and Poems
Beautiful Reflections: A Gift Of Poetry
In A Journey or Two: Inspirational Quotes

www.ajacotoripoetry.com

Email: ajacotori436@yahoo.com

Merry Christmas!

Merry Christmas!

Merry Christmas!

Made in the USA
Columbia, SC
17 November 2020